TABLE OF

———————❧·◆·❧———————

CHAPTER		PAGE #
1	THE SECRET PLACE IS THE PLACE YOU SET ASIDE TO MEET WITH THE HOLY SPIRIT EACH MORNING	3
2	UNCOMMON CHAMPIONS HAVE ALWAYS SET ASIDE A SPECIAL PLACE TO MEET WITH GOD	7
3	WHEN THE SECRET PLACE BECOMES YOUR MORNING HABIT, YOUR LIFE WILL EXPERIENCE DRAMATIC CHANGE	9
4	YOU MUST CLIMATIZE THE SECRET PLACE CONTINUALLY WITH ANOINTED MUSIC	13
5	THE SECRET PLACE IS WHERE THE HOLY SPIRIT REVEALS HIS SECRETS TO YOU	15
6	YOUR TIME IN THE SECRET PLACE IS THE PROOF OF YOUR DEPENDENCY UPON HIM	17
7	YOU MUST STAY LONG ENOUGH IN THE SECRET PLACE TO CREATE A MEMORY	19

Unless otherwise indicated, all Scripture quotations are taken from the King James Version of the Bible.
Where Miracles Are Born, Seeds of Wisdom on The Secret Place, Vol. 13
ISBN 1-56394-107-4/B-115
Copyright © 2001 by **MIKE MURDOCK**
All publishing rights belong exclusively to Wisdom International
Publisher/Editor: Deborah Murdock Johnson
Published by The Wisdom Center · 4051 Denton Hwy. · Ft. Worth, Texas 76117
1-817-759-Book · 1-817-759-2665 · 1-817-759-0300
You Will Love Our Website..! WisdomOnline.com

Uncommon People
Do Daily
What Common People
Do Occasionally.

-*MIKE MURDOCK*

❧ 1 ❧

THE SECRET PLACE IS THE PLACE YOU SET ASIDE TO MEET WITH THE HOLY SPIRIT EACH MORNING

Places Matter.

Places matter to God.

You see, He made places before He even made people! The first known Assignment for The Holy Spirit was to a *specific place.* "And the Spirit of God moved upon the face of the waters," (Genesis 1:2).

Jesus knew The Holy Spirit would appear and reveal Himself in a *specific place* (read 1 Corinthians 15:4-7 and Acts 1:2-4).

Jesus scheduled miracles to occur in *specific places* (John 4:4).

The instruction of Jesus to a blind man was to go to a *specific place* (John 9:1-7).

Naaman, the leper, was instructed by the prophet to dip in the Jordan River 7 times to receive his healing...*The Place of Obedience.*

Elijah was instructed to go to a *specific place,* for his financial provision (1 Kings 17).

Rebellion to enter The Place of Obedience always produces tragic results (Jonah 1).

So, nothing could be more important than The Secret Place...where you enter the Presence of God and become changed, corrected, informed and loved.

I have lived for more than half a century, preached 17,000 times in over 100 countries of the world. Yet, as of this writing, only 5 people in my lifetime have ever invited me to come and observe their private place of prayer, their "Secret Place." Many ministers have shown me gymnasiums, Sunday School rooms, sanctuaries and even $500,000 kitchens. *Only 5 have shown me their Secret Place.*

It is so important that you respect your daily companion, The Holy Spirit, enough to set aside a *specific place* of solitude and intimacy for Him to meet with you.

The Holy Spirit qualifies for exclusivity.

Though my private prayer room was established years before 1994, I fell in love with the Person of The Holy Spirit on Wednesday morning, at 7:00 a.m., July 13, 1994. That's the day that I would trade for every other day of my life.

Prior to that experience, I had not designated a specific room for The Holy Spirit. Neither had I named the room, "The Secret Place."

Before July 13, 1994, places had never really mattered much. From 15 years old, I traveled by bus to speak in churches across the United States. My first crusade was as a 15-year-old teenager.

Then, I attended Bible College for 3 semesters, and entered full-time evangelism on February 4, 1966, at the age of 19. That was 45 years ago.

Jesus often ministered to thousands. Yet, when He wanted to impart and create radical change in His disciples, He pulled them aside into a place of privacy (Mark 6:31).

The ministry of Jesus was explosive. It was powerful. Yet, He knew the Rewards of Solitude.

▶ Solitude is necessary for *intimacy.*

▶ Intimacy is necessary for *impartation*.

▶ Impartation is necessary for *change*.

You, too, must move away from the voices of others...to distinguish His Voice.

▶ Withdraw from the crowds.

▶ Disconnect from the demands of parasitic relationships.

▶ Depart from deceptive influences.

Create this very day a private place, sanctified and exclusive for the incredible relationship between you and the One Who created you, The Holy Spirit (Job 33:4).

Nothing is more important.

RECOMMENDED INVESTMENTS:
The Mentor's Manna on The Secret Place (Book/B-78/32 pg)
The Holy Spirit Handbook (Book/B-100/153 pg)
The 3 Most Important Things In Your Life (Book/B-101/240 pg)
The Holy Spirit Handbook (CD/CDS-29)

God Never Responds
To Pain,
But He Always Responds
To Pursuit.

-MIKE MURDOCK

❧ 2 ❧

UNCOMMON CHAMPIONS HAVE ALWAYS SET ASIDE A SPECIAL PLACE TO MEET WITH GOD

Champions Do What Others Refuse To Do.

Jacob had a special place where he experienced God. (See Genesis 35:13-15.) He even *named* his place, Bethel.

I encourage you to do the same. You may call your place of prayer...

▶ The Room of Hope...
▶ The Upper Room...
▶ The High Place...
▶ The Holy Chamber...
▶ The Secret Place.

Just name it!

Daniel, the incredible statesman of Wisdom, established a place of prayer. Even his enemies were aware of his place of prayer. (See Daniel 6:10.)

David, the psalmist, who was a man after God's own heart, had a special place of prayer and entered there *habitually*—7 times a day! (See Psalm 119:164.)

Jesus had special places for prayer, when He pulled aside from the multitudes. (See Mark 14:32, 35.)

History records that the great preachers such as John Wesley, George Whitefield and Charles G. Finny had specific *times* of prayer, *early* each morning.

So, when you follow the patterns and conduct of

champions who defied the darkness and opened the windows of Heaven on earth—they were Champions of Prayer who had *places* and *times* where they were mentored by The Holy Spirit.

▶ Crowds will *fragment* your focus.

▶ Recreation often *diverts* your attention from destiny.

▶ Friends can *influence* you greatly.

▶ Enemies *demoralize.*

▶ Children *obligate.*

The Holy Spirit alone *transforms.*

That's why you must disconnect from the world of human influence...and enter the *Harbor of Divine Impartation—The Secret Place.*

RECOMMENDED INVESTMENTS:
The Uncommon Achiever (Book/B-133/128 pg)
Secrets of the Greatest Achievers Who Ever Lived, Series 1
  (CD/CDS-06)
Secrets of the Greatest Achievers Who Ever Lived, Series 2
  (CD/CDS-07)

WHEN THE SECRET PLACE BECOMES YOUR MORNING HABIT, YOUR LIFE WILL EXPERIENCE DRAMATIC CHANGE

Ritual Matters.

God is ceremonial. He is ritualistic. He did not create us to be creatures of discipline, but rather creatures of *Habit.*

The Purpose of Discipline Is To Birth A Habit. When you perform the same action or task 30 consecutive days, it becomes a Habit.

The psalmist prayed 7 times a day.

Daniel prayed 3 times a day.

Jesus, *as was His custom*, went to the synagogue regularly.

Uncommon Achievers Do *Daily* What Common Men Do *Occasionally*.

Whenever you fail in your life, that failure can be traced to something that was occurring *daily* in your mind, home or life.

Whenever you succeed in your life, that success can be traced to something occurring *daily* in your mind, home or life.

- ▶ Men do not really decide their future—they decide their *focus*.
- ▶ Focus creates their *habits*.
- ▶ Habits determine their *future*.

Someone asked me, "Is it really necessary to enter The Secret Place and meet with The Holy Spirit in the *morning* time? Is night time just as effective?"

Any moment in His presence can change you. However, most people plan their trips *before* they take them. Why enter a day without His presence, His peace, His power? Certainly you can pray any time, effectively. Jesus even prayed entire nights. But, when you read the habits of men such as Abraham, Moses and Joshua...they arose *early*. (See Genesis 19:27; Exodus 34:4; Joshua 6:12.)

David said, *"Early will I seek Thee:* my soul thirsteth for Thee, my flesh longeth for Thee in a dry and thirsty land, where no water is; To see Thy power and Thy glory, so as I have seen Thee in the sanctuary," (Psalm 63:1-2).

The psalmist even prayed at *night.* "When I remember Thee upon my bed, and meditate on Thee in the night watches. Because Thou hast been my help, therefore in the shadow of Thy wings will I rejoice," (Psalm 63:6-7).

3 Important Keys

1. Set An Achievable Goal. Don't focus on getting up one hour earlier. Focus on arising 15 minutes earlier. Why? Remember the old saying— "How do you eat an elephant? A bite at a time."

2. Collect Daily Successes. Build on your prayer life. Start with something obtainable. You can always add from there. So many people set impossible goals for themselves. Doing so, they create memories of failures instead of memories of successes.

3. Educate Those Around You About Your New Prayer Time. They will cooperate with you and even be encouraged by it. Occasionally, they will even join you in your time of prayer. Nothing is more memorable than to observe your passion for The Holy Spirit.

What You Do Daily Determines What You Become Permanently.

RECOMMENDED INVESTMENTS:
The Holy Spirit Handbook (Book/B-100/153 pg)
The Holy Spirit Handbook (CD/CDS-29)

A Song
Is The Protocol
For Entering
The Presence of God.

-MIKE MURDOCK

4

YOU MUST CLIMATIZE THE SECRET PLACE CONTINUALLY WITH ANOINTED MUSIC

Atmosphere Matters.

The Holy Spirit instructed us concerning the protocol for entering His presence. "Come before His presence with singing...Enter into His gates with thanksgiving, and into His courts with praise: be thankful unto Him, and bless His name," (Psalm 100:2, 4). So, always enter The Secret Place singing.

The Holy Spirit loves music. His music. His songs. He responds to worship, singing and anointed musicians who honor Him.

Holy Spirit music often dispels evil spirits. King Saul was a very egotistical and sad king. But, he had memories of the presence of God. He knew enough about the anointing to call for David to create the climate for change. "And it came to pass, when the evil spirit from God was upon Saul, that David took an harp, and played with his hand: so Saul was refreshed, and was well, and *the evil spirit departed* from him," (1 Samuel 16:23).

I keep music playing continuously in my home. I have sound speakers on the trees outside in my yard. I have placed sound speakers throughout the various rooms of my house...so The Holy Spirit will hear what He requested—praise and worship.

There are no other distractions in my Secret

Place. No telephones. No fax machines. No walls fill-ed with books. No beds.

It is a Place for Divine Impartation.

I have *altars* in my Secret Place. I keep olive oil for anointing, water for drinking, a bulletin board with pictures of those for whom I am praying. I even keep Pictorial Prayer Books where I lay hands on the pictures of my partners and their families and intercede for them. Notebooks are handy to document the revelations of The Holy Spirit. I keep several Bibles on the altars.

My Secret Place is so strong with His presence that I have often had dear friends burst into tears when they entered the room. One well-known pastor wept and told me, as he left my Secret Place at 4:20 a.m., "I have never felt the presence of God like this in my entire lifetime."

In the famous movie, "Field of Dreams," someone said, "If you build it, they will come."

If you build a place for Him, The Holy Spirit will come. *What You Respect, You Will Attract.*

RECOMMENDED INVESTMENT:
The Mentor's Manna on The Secret Place (Book/B-78/32 pg)

THE SECRET PLACE IS WHERE THE HOLY SPIRIT REVEALS HIS SECRETS TO YOU

Where You Are Determines What You Hear.

At a football game, you will hear football players, cheerleaders and fans.

At a concert, you will hear musicians and songs.

At a zoo, you will hear the screams and sounds of exotic animals.

In The Secret Place, you will hear the intimate conversation of The Holy Spirit to you. "The secret of the Lord is with them that fear Him; and He will shew them His covenant," (Psalm 25:14).

4 Secrets The Holy Spirit Reveals

1. The Holy Spirit Will Reveal Changes In Your Assignment. (See 1 Samuel 3:8-13; Acts 8.)

2. The Holy Spirit Will Reveal The Weaknesses of Your Enemies. "Thou through Thy commandments hast made me wiser than mine enemies," (Psalm 119:98).

3. The Holy Spirit Will Reveal Where Your Gifts Are Most Needed. (See Acts 13:2-4.)

4. The Voice of The Holy Spirit Will Create Strength Within You. "And when He had spoken unto me, I was strengthened," (Daniel 10:19).

The Secret Place is the room you have set apart to receive revelation regarding your Assignment, your decisions and the plan of God for your life.

10 Miracles That Happen In The Secret Place

- ▶ It is the Room of *Hope*...where Impossibility Thinking becomes Possibility Thinking as you gaze upon the countenance of the One Who created you (Philippians 4:13).
- ▶ It is the Room of *Love*...where the love of God is poured into you for others to receive from you (1 John 4:16).
- ▶ It is the Room of *Change*...where hardened hearts become softened (Job 23:16).
- ▶ It is the Room of *Forgiveness*...where every mistake you have made is removed (Psalm 103:12).
- ▶ It is the Room of *Mercy*...where the guilt of sin is dissolved (Psalm 37:26).
- ▶ It is the Room of *Decision-Making*...where accurate information is imparted, making quality decisions possible (Psalm 32:8).
- ▶ It is the Room of *Financial Recovery*...where God's plan of survival becomes understood (Psalm 34:6).
- ▶ It is the Room of *Wisdom*...where the Law of God is forever engraved on your heart (Proverbs 4:7).
- ▶ It is the Room of *Waiting*...where the Seeds of Patience bear fruit (Isaiah 40:19-31).
- ▶ It is the Room of *Joy*...where He rewards the obedient with the fragrance called Joy (Psalm 16:11).

Those who invest time in The Secret Place are rewarded with the secrets of God.

YOUR TIME IN THE SECRET PLACE IS THE PROOF OF YOUR DEPENDENCY UPON HIM

Prayerlessness Proves Arrogance.

When I fail to enter The Secret Place, my pride and self-sufficiency has been *documented.*

The Holy Spirit wants me...

▶ to be *aware* of my inability,

▶ to be *trusting* of His counsel,

▶ to be *addicted* to His presence.

That's why having a specific place for your morning appointment with Him is so vital and necessary.

"But, I pray every morning in my bedroom!" one upset Christian lady exclaimed. "What's wrong with simply praying in my bedroom?"

"You do everything else in the bedroom," I replied. "You watch television, phone your friends and sleep. The Holy Spirit deserves exclusivity."

When I delay entering The Secret Place at my home, I can almost visualize The Holy Spirit standing at the door stating calmly but urgently, "You have not sought *Me.* You have not reached for *Me.* You are trying to do everything without pursuing My counsel. Nothing succeeds without Me."

Thinking is not praying.

Worrying is not praying.

Discussing problems is not praying.

You need a Secret Place just for Him.

Memory Is
    The Miracle Map
Divinely Designed
    To Rediscover
Places of Pleasure.

-MIKE MURDOCK

7

YOU MUST STAY LONG ENOUGH IN THE SECRET PLACE TO CREATE A MEMORY

Satan Cannot Steal Your Memories.

That was the secret revealed in the sensational return of the prodigal to his father's house.

His money was stolen.

His friends were gone.

His self-confidence was shattered.

But, his memories remained.

> ▶ *Memory Is The Miracle Magnet...Attracting You Back To Your Father's House.*
> ▶ *Memory Is The Gift of God Linking You To Your Restoration.*
> ▶ *Memory Is The Catalyst For Repentance.*

You will only return to a Place of Pleasure.

So, you must stay long enough in The Secret Place to create a memory of pleasure, change and strength. If you leave too soon, before The Holy Spirit talks to you, you may become reluctant to return.

How Long Should You Stay?

> ▶ *Stay long enough to receive His command.* "Therefore Thou shalt keep the commandments of the Lord thy God, to walk in His ways, and to fear Him," (Deuteronomy 8:6).
> ▶ *Stay long enough for Hope to be birthed again.* "My soul fainteth for Thy salvation: but I

hope in Thy Word," (Psalm 119:81).

▶ *Stay long enough to become broken.* "The Lord is nigh unto them that are of a broken heart; and saveth such as be of a contrite spirit," (Psalm 34:18).

▶ *Stay long enough to recapture your motivation.* "I can do all things through Christ which strengtheneth me," (Philippians 4:13).

▶ *Stay long enough for new ideas to be birthed.* "But my God shall supply all your need according to His riches in glory by Christ Jesus," (Philippians 4:19).

▶ *Stay long enough to be changed.* "And was transfigured before them: and His face did shine as the sun, and His raiment was white as the light," (Matthew 17:2).

▶ *Stay long enough to receive His Wisdom.* "I will instruct thee and teach thee in the way which thou shalt go: I will guide thee with Mine eye," (Psalm 32:8).

▶ *Stay long enough to become stronger.* "But they that wait upon the Lord shall renew their strength; they shall mount up with wings as eagles; they shall run, and not be weary; and they shall walk, and not faint," (Isaiah 40:31).

▶ *Stay long enough to receive His Complete Plan for achieving your goal.* "For I know the thoughts that I think toward you, saith the Lord, thoughts of peace, and not of evil, to give you an expected end," (Jeremiah 29:11).

▶ *Stay long enough for mistakes to be exposed.* "He that covereth his sins shall not prosper: but whoso confesseth and forsaketh them shall have mercy," (Proverbs 28:13).

▶ *Stay long enough for pain to leave.* "...weeping

may endure for a night, but joy cometh in the morning," (Psalm 30:5).

▶ *Stay long enough for confusion to disappear.* "For God is not the Author of confusion, but of peace," (1 Corinthians 14:33).

▶ *Stay long enough for love to emerge again.* "And hope maketh not ashamed: because the love of God is shed abroad in our hearts by the Holy Ghost which is given unto us," (Romans 5:5).

▶ *Stay long enough for the spirit of murmuring and complaining to dissipate.* "Do all things without murmurings and disputings," (Philippians 2:14).

▶ *Stay long enough to receive contentment.* "Not that I speak in respect of want: for I have learned, in whatsoever state I am, therewith to be content," (Philippians 4:11).

▶ *Stay long enough to lavish love on Him.* "But whoso keepeth His word, in him verily is the love of God perfected: hereby know we that we are in Him," (1 John 2:5).

▶ *Stay long enough to read His Word aloud.* "My tongue shall speak of Thy word: for all Thy commandments are righteousness," (Psalm 119:172).

▶ *Stay long enough to listen to His Word.* "So then faith cometh by hearing, and hearing by the word of God," (Romans 10:17).

▶ *Stay long enough to meditate on Him.* "O how love I Thy law! it is my meditation all the day," (Psalm 119:97).

▶ *Stay long enough to intercede for your family members.* Lay your hands on their pictures in your pictorial prayer book. "Moreover as for me, God forbid that I should sin against the

Lord in ceasing to pray for you: but I will teach you the good and the right way," (1 Samuel 12:23).

► *Stay long enough for your anger to subside.* "He that hath no rule over his own spirit is like a city that is broken down, and without walls," (Proverbs 25:28).

► *Stay long enough for the fear of man to dissolve and leave.* "The fear of man bringeth a snare: but whoso putteth his trust in the Lord shall be safe," (Proverbs. 29:25).

► *Stay long enough for true joy to return.* "Thou wilt shew me the path of life: in Thy presence is fulness of joy; at Thy right hand there are pleasures for evermore," (Psalm 16:11).

Always Exit The Secret Place With Expectation... *Nothing Will Occur Today That You And The Holy Spirit Cannot Handle Together.*

Our Closing Prayer Together...

"Holy Spirit, unleash a new passion for Your presence in my dear reader today. Schedule a visitation that will be impossible for them to ever doubt. In Jesus' name. Amen."

DECISION

Will You Accept Jesus As Your Personal Savior Today?

The Bible says, "That if thou shalt confess with thy mouth the Lord Jesus, and shalt believe in thine heart that God hath raised Him from the dead, thou shalt be saved," (Romans 10:9).

Pray this prayer from your heart today!

"Dear Jesus, I believe that You died for me and rose again on the third day. I confess I am a sinner...I need Your love and forgiveness...Come into my heart. Forgive my sins. I receive Your eternal life. Confirm Your love by giving me peace, joy and supernatural love for others. Amen."

DR. MIKE MURDOCK

is in tremendous demand as one of the most dynamic speakers in America today.

More than 17,000 audiences in over 100 countries have attended his conferences and Schools of Wisdom. Hundreds of invitations come to him from churches, colleges and business corporations. He is a noted author of over 250 books, including the best sellers, *The Leadership Secrets of Jesus* and *Secrets of the Richest Man Who Ever Lived.* Thousands view his weekly television program, *Wisdom Keys with Mike Murdock.* Many attend his Schools of Wisdom that he hosts in major cities of America.

☐ Yes, Mike, I made a decision to accept Christ as my personal Savior today. Please send me my free gift of your book, *31 Keys to a New Beginning* to help me with my new life in Christ.

NAME   BIRTHDAY

ADDRESS

CITY   STATE   ZIP

PHONE   E-MAIL

Mail form to:
The Wisdom Center · 4051 Denton Hwy. · Ft. Worth, TX 76117
1-817-759-BOOK · 1-817-759-2665 · 1-817-759-0300
You Will Love Our Website..! WisdomOnline.com   23

JOIN THE

Wisdom Key 3000

TODAY!

Will You Become My Ministry Partner In The Work of God?

Dear Friend,

God has connected us!

I have asked The Holy Spirit for 3000 Special Partners who will plant a monthly Seed of $58.00 to help me bring the gospel around the world. (58 represents 58 kinds of blessings in the Bible.)

Will you become my monthly Faith Partner in The Wisdom Key 3000? Your monthly Seed of $58.00 is so powerful in helping heal broken lives. When you sow into the work of God, 4 Miracle Harvests are guaranteed in Scripture, Isaiah 58...

- ▸ Uncommon Health (Isaiah 58)
- ▸ Uncommon Wisdom For Decision-Making (Isaiah 58)
- ▸ Uncommon Financial Favor (Isaiah 58)
- ▸ Uncommon Family Restoration (Isaiah 58)

Your Faith Partner,

Mike Murdock

P.S. Please clip the coupon attached and return it to me today, so I can rush the Wisdom Key Partnership Pak to you... or call me at 1-817-759-0300.

Thank You For Joining
The Wisdom Key 3000!

THE CRAZIEST instruct Go
EVER GAVE
The Personal Testimony
Unlocks Miracles F...
MIKE MURDOCK

THE Covenant OF Fifty-Ei Blessin

10 WISD KEY

The Blessing BIBLE

WISDOM KEY 3000 PARTNERSHIP SEED BOOK

PP-03

The Wisdom and Miracle of the 58th...
Wisdom Key 3000
MIKE MURDOCK

365 Memory Scriptures on The Word of God
Wisdom Key 3000
MIKE MURDOCK

MIKE MURDOCK Music Library
Wisdom Key 3000 Edition

☐ *Yes, Mike, I want to join The Wisdom Key 3000.*
   Please rush The Wisdom Key Partnership Pak to me today!
☐ *Enclosed is my first monthly Seed-Faith Promise of:*
   ☐ *$58* ☐ *Other $_____.*

☐HECK ☐MONEY ORDER ☐AMEX ☐DISCOVER ☐MASTERCARD ☐VISA

dit Card # _____ Exp. ____/____

nature _____

me _____ Birth Date ____/____

ress _____

_____ State _____ Zip _____

one _____ E-Mail _____

WK304

THE WISDOM CENTER
4051 Denton Highway • Fort Worth, TX 76117

1-817-759-BOOK
1-817-759-2665
1-817-759-0300

— You Will Love Our Website..! —
WisdomOnline.com 25

Salvation of Husband..!

I sowed $5.80 three weeks ago, I received a $249 check, now I am sowing $58 x 2 = $116 in my church, and I gave a command to my Seed for the 1,000 times more. Today my husband received the Lord in my church in Vega Baja, this is one of the miracles I was looking for in 58 days.

N. - Puerto RIco

Changes In Alzheimer's Disease..!

When you were at our church in Baltimore, in March of this year, I planted a $58 Seed for my mother's health and well-being. She will be 97 years old on May 27th and the doctor said Alzheimer's. We did not accept that diagnosis. About three weeks ago, we began to see and hear such a dramatic change in my mother that I know, and my family agrees, that God moved on her behalf. We expect her to have many more fruitful years.

B. - Baltimore, MD

Childless Couple Receives Baby Boy As "The Harvest"..!

In the Fall, we planted a $58 Seed-Assignment to have a child. We had been told by three specialists that I couldn't have children. Nine months later I had a 9 lb. 4 oz. bouncing boy.

H.

Protection In Auto Accident..!

I met you here in New York several months ago, and I planted a $58 Seed then and God has blessed me. On August 15th, I was in an automobile accident. The car flipped over twice, I think, but I am still alive and didn't suffer any injuries. Praise God!

A. - Bronx, NY

$14,000 Miracle..!

I had sent in a check for $58 on the 58 Covenant of Blessings. That day we received a check for $5,000 in the mail and a promise from my in-laws to pay off the rest of our land...mortgage at the bank for over $14,000. Praise the Lord!   **C. - LaPorte, IN**

New Car..!

I attend church in Sarasota, Florida. You were here at the beginning of this year and asked for a $58 Seed.

I have been believing for a new car for some time now. I sowed a Seed and thirteen days later someone came to me completely unexpected and said they would buy me any car I wanted.

Our Youth Pastor was also blessed with a car and another single lady in the church had the same blessing (these are just the ones I know about.)

Thank you for being a part of the "new car" anointing here at Victory. God bless you and your loved ones.   **D. - Bradenton, FL**

From $50,000 A Year To $80,000..!

My husband and I heard you speak about the $58 blessing on T.V. The first month we named the Seed for our younger son. He went from $50,000 a year to $80,000 income change in one day basically. He took a random phone call at work from a headhunter and changed jobs. Anyone could have answered that phone!

M. & G. - Farmerville, TX

DR. MIKE MURDOCK

1 Has embraced his Assignment to Pursue...Proclaim...and Publish the Wisdom of God to help people achieve their dreams and goals.

2 Preached his first public sermon at the age of 8.

3 Preached his first evangelistic crusade at the age of 15.

4 Began full-time evangelism at the age of 19, which has continued since 1966.

5 Has traveled and spoken to more than 17,000 audiences in over 100 countries, including East and West Africa, Asia, Europe and South America.

6 Noted author of over 250 books, including best sellers, *Wisdom for Winning*, *Dream Seeds*, *The Double Diamond Principle, The Law of Recognition* and *The Holy Spirit Handbook.*

7 Created the popular *Topical Bible* series for Businessmen, Mothers, Fathers, Teenagers; *The One-Minute Pocket Bible* series, and *The Uncommon Life* series.

8 The Creator of The Master 7 Mentorship System, an Achievement Program for Believers.

9 Has composed thousands of songs such as "I Am Blessed," "You Can Make It," "God Rides On Wings of Love" and "Jesus, Just The Mention of Your Name," recorded by many gospel artists.

10 Is the Founder and Senior Pastor of The Wisdom Center, in Fort Worth, Texas...a Church with International Ministry around the world.

11 Host of *Wisdom Keys with Mike Murdock,* a weekly TV Program seen internationally.

12 Has appeared often on TBN, CBN, BET, Daystar, Inspirational Network, LeSea Broadcasting and other television network programs.

13 Has led over 3,000 to accept the call into full-time ministry.

THE MINISTRY

1 **Wisdom Books & Literature** - Over 250 best-selling Wisdom Books and 70 Teaching Tape Series.

2 **Church Crusades** - Multitudes are ministered to in crusades and seminars throughout America in "The Uncommon Wisdom Conferences." Known as a man who loves pastors, he has focused on church crusades for over 43 years.

3 **Music Ministry** - Millions have been blessed by the anointed songwriting and singing of Mike Murdock, who has made over 15 music albums and CDs available.

4 **Television** - *Wisdom Keys with Mike Murdock,* a nationally-syndicated weekly television program.

5 **The Wisdom Center** - The Church and Ministry Offices where Dr. Murdock speaks weekly on Wisdom for The Uncommon Life.

6 **Schools of The Holy Spirit** - Mike Murdock hosts Schools of The Holy Spirit in many churches to mentor believers on the Person and Companionship of The Holy Spirit.

7 **Schools of Wisdom** - In many major cities Mike Murdock hosts Schools of Wisdom for those who want personalized and advanced training for achieving "The Uncommon Dream."

8 **Missions Outreach** - Dr. Mike Murdock's overseas outreaches to over 100 countries have included crusades in East and West Africa, Asia, Europe and South America.

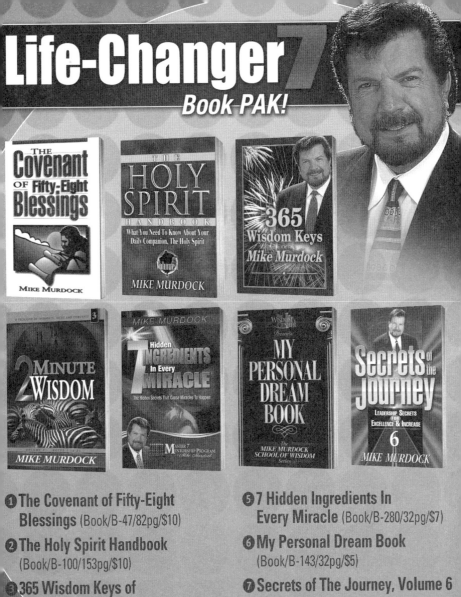

Life-Changer 7 Book PAK!

① **The Covenant of Fifty-Eight Blessings** (Book/B-47/82pg/$10)

② **The Holy Spirit Handbook** (Book/B-100/153pg/$10)

③ **365 Wisdom Keys of Mike Murdock** (Book/B-229/64pg/$15)

④ **2 Minute Wisdom, Volume 3** (Book/B-248/32pg/$7)

⑤ **7 Hidden Ingredients In Every Miracle** (Book/B-280/32pg/$7)

⑥ **My Personal Dream Book** (Book/B-143/32pg/$5)

⑦ **Secrets of The Journey, Volume 6** (Book/B-102/32pg/$5)

The Wisdom Center
All 7 Books for only
$**20** $59 Value
PAK-50
Wisdom Is The Principal Thing

All 7 Books For One Great Price!

Each Wisdom Book may be purchased separately if so desired.

Add 20% For S/H

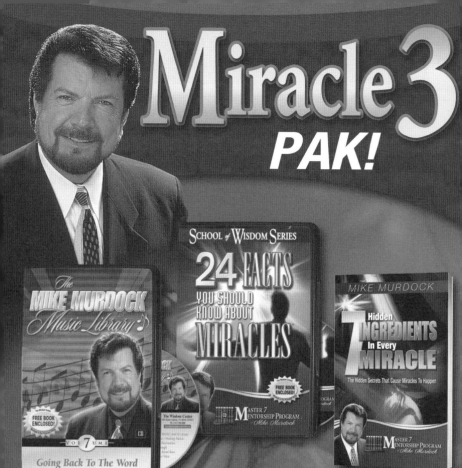

Miracle 3 PAK!

1 **Going Back To The Word** (CD/MMML-07)
.......*Free Book Included With Music CD.*

2 **24 Facts You Should Know About Miracles** (CD/WCPL-158)
.......*Free Book Included With CD.*

3 **7 Hidden Ingredients In Every Miracle** (Book/B-280/32pg)

*Each Wisdom Product may be purchased separately if so desired.

The Wisdom Center
Miracle 3 Pak!
Only $**20** $33 Value
PAK-46
Wisdom Is The Principal Thing

Add 20% For S/H

THE WISDOM CENTER
4051 Denton Highway · Fort Worth, TX 76117

1-817-759-BOOK
1-817-759-2665
1-817-759-0300

— You Will Love Our Website..! —
WisdomOnline.com

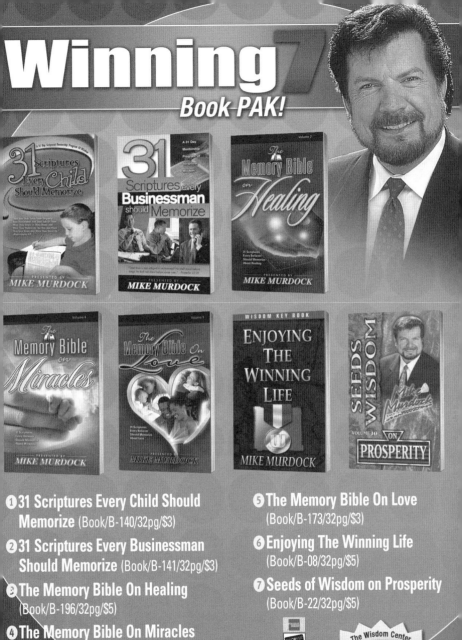

Winning 7 Book PAK!

① **31 Scriptures Every Child Should Memorize** (Book/B-140/32pg/$3)

② **31 Scriptures Every Businessman Should Memorize** (Book/B-141/32pg/$3)

③ **The Memory Bible On Healing** (Book/B-196/32pg/$5)

④ **The Memory Bible On Miracles** (Book/B-208/32pg/$3)

⑤ **The Memory Bible On Love** (Book/B-173/32pg/$3)

⑥ **Enjoying The Winning Life** (Book/B-08/32pg/$5)

⑦ **Seeds of Wisdom on Prosperity** (Book/B-22/32pg/$5)

The Wisdom Center
All 7 Books for only $15 $27 Value
PAK-51
Wisdom Is The Principal Thing

All 7 Books For One Great Price!

Each Wisdom Book may be purchased separately if so desired.

Add 20% For S/H

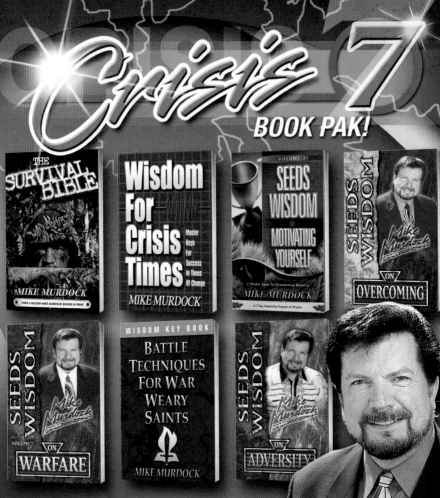

Crisis 7 BOOK PAK!

DR. MIKE MURDOCK

❶ **The Survival Bible** (Book/B-29/248pg/$10)

❷ **Wisdom For Crisis Times** (Book/B-40/112pg/$9)

❸ **Seeds of Wisdom on Motivating Yourself** (Book/B-171/32pg/$5)

❹ **Seeds of Wisdom on Overcoming** (Book/B-17/32pg/$3)

❺ **Seeds of Wisdom on Warfare** (Book/B-19/32pg/$5)

❻ **Battle Techniques For War-Weary Saints** (Book/B-07/32pg/$5)

❼ **Seeds of Wisdom on Adversity** (Book/B-21/32pg/$3)

The Wisdom Center
Crisis 7 Book Pak!
Only $30 $40 Value
WBL-25
Wisdom Is The Principal Thing

Add 20% For S/H

Quantity Prices Available Upon Request

Each Wisdom Book may be purchased separately if so desired.

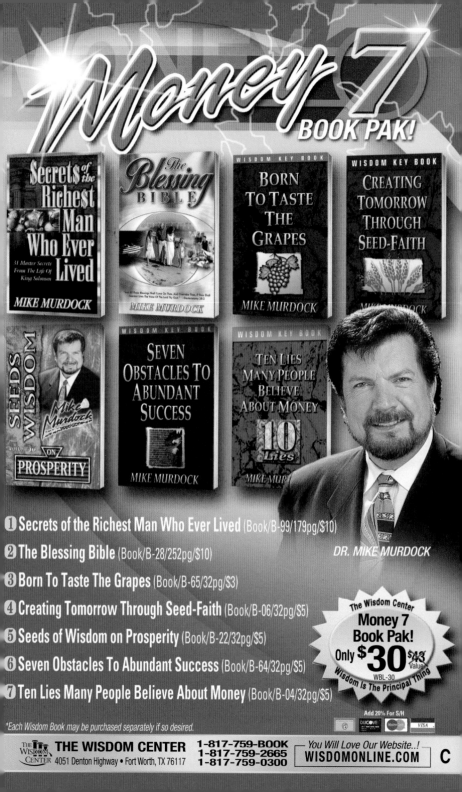

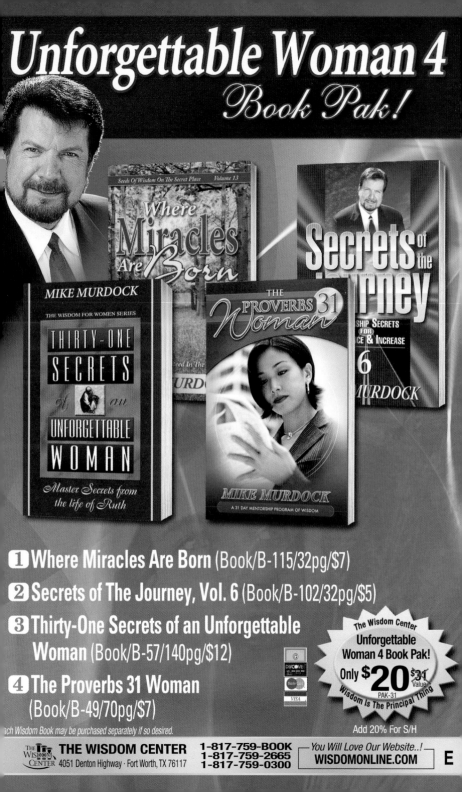

Unforgettable Woman 4
Book Pak!

1 Where Miracles Are Born (Book/B-115/32pg/$7)

2 Secrets of The Journey, Vol. 6 (Book/B-102/32pg/$5)

3 Thirty-One Secrets of an Unforgettable Woman (Book/B-57/140pg/$12)

4 The Proverbs 31 Woman (Book/B-49/70pg/$7)

The Wisdom Center
Unforgettable
Woman 4 Book Pak!
Only $20 $31 Value
PAK-31
Wisdom Is The Principal Thing

ach Wisdom Book may be purchased separately if so desired.

Add 20% For S/H

The Businessman's Devotional 4 Book Pak!

❶ 7 Rewards of Problem Solving (Book/B-118/32pg/$8)

❷ My Personal Dream Book (Book/B-143/32pg/$5)

❸ 1 Minute Businessman's Devotional
(Book/B-42/224pg/$12)

❹ 31 Greatest Chapters In The Bible
(Book/B-54/138pg/$10)

The Wisdom Center
The Businessman's Devotional 4 Book Pak!
Only $**20** $35 Value
PAK-22
Wisdom Is The Principal Thing

Add 20% For S/H

Millionaire-Talk

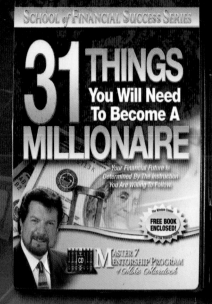

DR. MIKE MURDOCK

31 Things You Will Need To Become A Millionaire (2-CD's/WCPL-116)

Topics Include:

- You Will Need Financial Heroes
- Your Willingness To Negotiate Everything
- You Must Have The Ability To Transfer Your Enthusiasm, Your Vision To Others
- Know Your Competition
- Be Willing To Train Your Team Personally As To Your Expectations
- Hire Professionals To Do A Professional's Job

I have asked the Lord for 3,000 special partners who will sow an extra Seed of $58 towards our Television Outreach Ministry. Your Seed is so appreciated! Remember to request your Gift CD's, 2 Disc Volume, *31 Things You Will Need To Become A Millionaire,* when you write this week!

THE WISDOM CENTER
4051 Denton Highway • Fort Worth, TX 76117

1-817-759-BOOK
1-817-759-2665
1-817-759-0300

You Will Love Our Website..!
WISDOMONLINE.COM

G

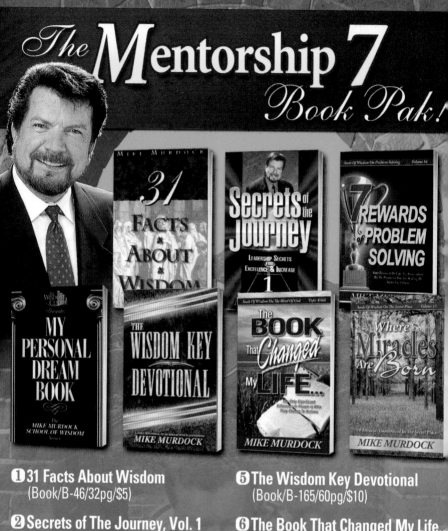

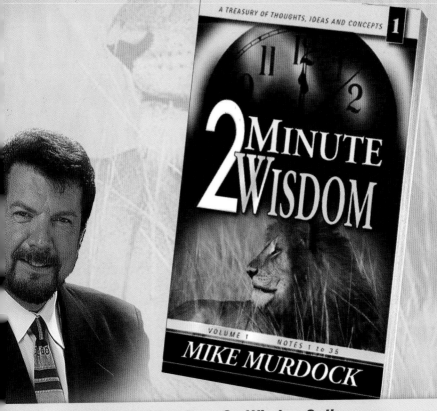

THE WISDOM BIBLE

Partnership Edition

Over 120 Wisdom Study Guides Included Such As:

- ▶ *10 Qualities of Uncommon Achievers*
- ▶ *18 Facts You Should Know About The Anointing*
- ▶ *21 Facts To Help You Identify Those Assigned To You*
- ▶ *31 Facts You Should Know About Your Assignment*
- ▶ *8 Keys That Unlock Victory In Every Attack*
- ▶ *22 Defense Techniques To Remember During Seasons of Personal Attack*
- ▶ *20 Wisdom Keys And Techniques To Remember During An Uncommon Battle*
- ▶ *11 Benefits You Can Expect From God*
- ▶ *31 Facts You Should Know About Favor*
- ▶ *The Covenant of 58 Blessings*
- ▶ *7 Keys To Receiving Your Miracle*
- ▶ *16 Facts You Should Remember About Contentious People*
- ▶ *5 Facts Solomon Taught About Contracts*
- ▶ *7 Facts You Should Know About Conflict*
- ▶ *6 Steps That Can Unlock Your Self-Confidence*
- ▶ *And Much More!*

Your Partnership makes such a difference in The Wisdom Center Outreach Ministries. I wanted to place a Gift in your hand that could last a lifetime for you and your family...**The Wisdom Study Bible.**

40 Years of Personal Notes...this Partnership Edition Bible contains 160 pages of my Personal Study Notes...that could forever change your Bible Study of The Word of God. This **Partnership Edition...**is my personal **Gift of Appreciation** when you sow your Sponsorship Seed of $1,000 for our Television Outreach Ministry. An Uncommon Seed Always Creates An Uncommon Harvest!

Mike

Thank you from my heart for your Seed of Obedience (Luke 6:38).

This Gift of Appreciation Will Change Your Bible Study For The Rest of Your Life.

The Wisdom Bible

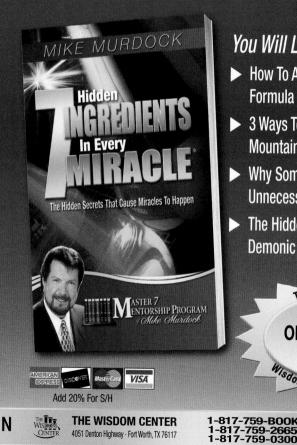

YOUR ASSIGNMENT IS YOUR DISTINCTION FROM OTHERS.

Assignment 4 Book Pak!

Uncommon Wisdom For Discovering Your Life Assignment.

❶ The Dream & The Destiny
Vol 1 (Book/B-74/164 pg/$15)

❷ The Anointing & The Adversity
Vol 2 (Book/B-75/192 pg/$10)

❸ The Trials & The Triumphs
Vol 3 (Book/B-97/160 pg/$10)

❹ The Pain & The Passion
Vol 4 (Book/B-98/144 pg/$10)

Each Wisdom Book may be purchased separately if so desired.

The Wisdom Center
Assignment 4 Book Pak!
Only $**30** $45 Value
WBL-14
Wisdom Is The Principal Thing

Add 20% For S/H